Reinvent Your Life
The Communication Skills of Highly Successful People

Table of Contents

Chapter 1. Introduction

Dive headfirst into an ocean of transformation with our energetic and empowering Special Report: "Reinvent Your Life: The Communication Skills of Highly Successful People". This resource is not just a collection of words, it's an enlightening journey that will show you the secret channels successful people use to communicate their ideas effectively. Not technical or dull, but riveting and filled with powerful, practical advice, these game-changing strategies are gleaned from the wisdom of the world's most successful people and are guaranteed to help you reinvent your life. So, ready to step onto a path that leads straight to success? Your journey of reinvention starts here!

Chapter 2. Unlocking the Power of Effective Communication

Communication is the lifeline of any successful relationship or endeavor. However, many struggle, not for the lack of knowledge or technical skills, but the inability to communicate effectively. Here are key concepts and guidelines you should grasp thoroughly to enhance your communication skills and influence others positively.

2.1. Understanding Communication

Before we delve much deeper, it's vital to understand what communication entails. The process of communication isn't limited to the exchange of information. Instead, it encompasses the transmission of feelings, ideas, emotions, and thoughts. It's about making your ideas understood, influencing others, and creating a shared understanding.

Experts identify two primary types of communication: verbal and non-verbal. Verbal communication refers to the spoken or written word that you use to convey your thoughts. On the other hand, non-verbal communication revolves around gestures, body language, posture, tone of voice, facial expressions, and even the pause between words.

2.2. The Art of Listening

Listening is an underrated but critical part of effective communication. It requires more than simply hearing words spoken by another person. It's about understanding those words, processing them, and providing a meaningful response. Active, attentive listening helps prevent misinterpretation and misunderstanding of messages.

Practicing 'empathetic listening' could also drastically improve your communication prowess. This form of listening is when you strive to understand both the content of the person's conversation and their emotional state. It's a powerful way to display respect for another's viewpoint, even in disagreement, and goes a long way in developing trust and understanding.

2.3. Non-Verbal Communication

Non-verbal cues can provide a wealth of understanding about another person's thoughts and feelings. Body language, facial expressions, and gestures carry significant weight in the communication process. They can either reinforce verbal communication or negate it entirely.

Maintaining eye contact, utilizing open body language, modulating your voice appropriately and mindful use of gestures amplifies the effectiveness of your communication; it also portrays confidence and clarity of thought.

2.4. Enhancing Verbal Communication

Words reign supreme in communication. They have the power to create and destroy, encourage and demotivate, heal and harm. Therefore, it's crucial to select your words carefully and articulate your thoughts coherently.

Practicing clarity, conciseness, and cohesion in your speech can significantly enhance your message's delivery. Being clear avoids ambiguity; being concise keeps your audience's attention, and cohesion ties your ideas together for easier understanding.

2.5. The Power of Silence

Understanding the power of silence is another key facet to unlocking effective communication. Silence can be used strategically to allow the recipient time to absorb the information, reflect on it, and formulate a response.

When harnessed correctly, silence serves as a powerful tool for negotiation, persuasion, and influence.

2.6. Emotional Intelligence and Communication

Emotional intelligence plays a crucial role in crafting and interpreting messages effectively. By integrating empathy into our interactions, we can better understanding others' emotional states and respond appropriately.

Managing your emotions while communicating is also essential. Emotions have the potential to override rational thinking, leading to conflicts or miscommunications. Staying calm and composed will help ensure that your message is delivered and received effectively.

2.7. Final Thoughts

Unlocking the power of effective communication required patience, continuous practice, and self-awareness. Understanding the process and intricate details that define communication, practicing active listening, observing non-verbal cues, enhancing your verbal delivery, using silence effectively, and integrating emotional intelligence into your interactions are all critical elements of this process.

Remember, communication is an avenue for understanding, growth, and progress. Therefore, honing these skills could significantly impact your personal and professional life, giving you an edge in various social situations and facilitating the achievement of your most ambitious goals. By investing time and effort in enhancing your communication skills you are essentially investing in your future success.

Chapter 3. Mastering the Art of Nonverbal Communication

Nonverbal communication is a pivotal part of our everyday exchanges, often underrated and overlooked. Yet, it is a key facet of how successful people register their impact, gain meaningful insights about their audience, and shape their influence. This guide will delve into the heart of nonverbal communication, dissecting its fundamental elements, and enabling individuals to use it to reinvent their lives positively.

3.1. Importance of Nonverbal Communication

A cascade of studies show that the majority of our communication is nonverbal, which includes body language, vocal tone, facial expressions - elements we often pay little heed to in our daily interactions. Contrary to popular belief, words alone are not enough to convey our thoughts or grasp the feelings of others effectively. By understanding nonverbal cues, we open a new realm of communication, allowing for deeper connections and clearer articulation of our intentions.

A sudden glance, a silenced sigh, a discrete gesture - these can itemize more about someone's thoughts than words muttered. Hence, mastering nonverbal communication is not merely a desirable skill; it is an absolute necessity in our journey towards success.

3.2. Learning to Read Body Language

The first step in deciphering nonverbal cues is understanding body language. Body language can significantly reflect an individual's thoughts or emotional state, often revealing what words might mask.

Observe with intent how a person stands or sits. An upright posture exudes confidence, while slouching may indicate low self-esteem or disinterest. Crossed arms may signify defensive behavior, indicating discomfort or apprehension.

Similarly, facial expressions provide critical hints about a person's mood or mindset. For instance, a furrowed brow may denote confusion, arched eyebrows indicate surprise, and a tight-lipped smile often signals discomfort or disappointment.

Remember, it's not a standalone signal but rather, the convergence of multiple cues that help discern the correct interpretation of body language, leading to a more detailed understanding of the person.

3.3. Understanding Tone of Voice

Often, it's not what you say but how you say it. The tone of voice affects how our messages are received and interpreted. A higher pitch indicates excitement or panic, low pitch might suggest seriousness or sadness, while a steady, calm voice expresses confidence.

Speech speed can also be a nonverbal cue. A rapidly delivered statement might display nervousness or excitement, while a slow speech speed may be perceived as thoughtful or lost.

A successful person knows how people perceive their vocal tone and knows how to vary it according to the situation.

3.4. The Power of Eye Contact

In nonverbal communication, our eyes play an instrumental role. Eye contact can reflect attentiveness, alertness, and engagement. It establishes a connection, affirming the listener's participation in the conversation.

However, too much eye contact can make someone uncomfortable and may be perceived as a form of dominance or intimidation. On the flip side, too little eye contact could signify inattentiveness, boredom, or deceit. Therefore, it is crucial to strike a balanced approach to eye contact, ensuring it conveys respect and interest in the conversation.

3.5. The Significance of Personal Space

Understanding and respecting personal space is another facet of nonverbal communication that successful people practice effectively. An invasion of personal space, however unintentional, can make the other person uncomfortable or threatened.

Having a grasp of the cultural and personal differences in individuals' comfort zones can help navigate interpersonal relationships more effectively. In short, paying heed to personal space is just as paramount as being competent in verbal dialogue.

3.6. Use of Gestures

Like a dash of color on a blank canvas, gestures can turn a mundane conversation lively and engaging. Hand gestures can accentuate a point or direct attention, thus contributing to more cohesive and lively communication.

However, it's critical to gauge cultural differences in interpreting gestures. A gesture may be seen as respectful in one culture and offensive in another. Thus, knowledge and sensitivity to cultural nuances become essential in global communication.

3.7. Developing a Nonverbal Vocabulary

In essence, nonverbal communication is like developing a second language, a silent, powerful vocabulary that can augment your social dexterity exponentially. It needs constant practice and keen observation to be an effective nonverbal communicator.

Practicing in front of a mirror, taking conscious control of nonverbal cues during dialogue, and seeking feedback can help refine these skills.

Moreover, effective usage requires a heightened consciousness of others' nonverbal cues. This observational skill can be exercised by watching televised speeches, public interactions, or even day-to-day conversations, thus enriching your nonverbal repertoire.

The realm of nonverbal communication, as vast and deep as the ocean, is an indispensable tool in the arsenal of highly successful people. Mastering it can transform our lives, enhancing the impact of our words, connecting effortlessly with others, and making every interaction more meaningful, powerful, and fruitful. So embrace this hidden skill, practice it with conscious effort, and see the profound transformation that ensues in your journey towards success.

Chapter 4. Commanding Confidence: Self-Expression in the Modern World

Innovation, creativity, and leadership. You've heard these buzzwords in every corner of the professional and personal development world. However, what do they have in common? The absolute need for communication - a vigorous, unyielding, bold version of expressing yourself. But it all starts with commanding confidence, fostering in you, a knack of self-expression like never witnessed before.

4.1. Building Your Confidence

Confidence is a constellation of beliefs, and at the very core of that grouping is the belief in one's ability to express oneself effectively. It's a foundation upon which other beliefs are built. Understanding this, we realize that the journey to confidence begins by strengthening one's belief in self-expression.

Understanding, evaluating, and working on your personal communication patterns can drastically elevate your confidence level. A challenge? Perhaps. Insignificant? Definitely not. Remember, when you get your communication right, the world starts seeing you differently, and more importantly, you begin seeing yourself differently.

Acquiring knowledge and skills feeds your confidence and empowers self-expression. The more you get to know about your field of work, industry, hobbies, or any matter of interest, the more confident you become in expressing your viewpoints about those subjects. Gift yourself time each day to learn something new, or to get better in an area you're already familiar with.

4.2. The Power of Self-Expression

Self-expression isn't merely about voicing your opinions. It's a venue to express thoughts, feelings, ideas - an art that is so much more than words. Communicating confidently fuels this art. It can manifest itself in a philosophical discussion, a business meeting, an art piece, or even in your personal style.

The real power of self-expression lies in authenticity. No one else thinks, talks, or presents ideas the way you do. Your thoughts, your voice, your style – they form the unique code of your self-expression. Embracing this uniqueness gives you a stand-out presence in any professional or personal gathering.

Authenticity while expressing oneself attracts like-minded people and opens up opportunities that sync well with your true self. There's a ripple effect fostered by confidence: express confidently, attract positivity, amplify success.

4.3. The Technique Behind Effective Self-Expression

Now that we've understood the role of confidence and authenticity in self-expression, let's dive into the how. Here are several techniques that can make your communication more impactful.

1. **Preparation:** Spend time synthesizing your thoughts before expressing them. It helps you articulate better and enhances your confidence.

2. **Clarity:** Be lucid and specific in your communication. Clarity helps others understand your point of view better, enhancing the quality of further conversation.

3. **Non-verbal cues**: Your body language, posture, gaze, and smile can speak volumes. Make sure they align with the message you're

trying to communicate.

4. **Empathy:** Understand the emotional landscape of your conversation, and adapt accordingly. This enhances the connection between the speaker and the listener.

5. **Feedback:** Constructive feedback gives you a chance to explore the effectiveness of your communication and make necessary changes.

6. **Consistency:** Develop a consistent pattern. Consistency is not just about the frequency of communication but also about the quality.

4.4. The Impact of Confidence in Communication

Imagine a situation where you converse with ease, express your ideas clearly, and leave a lasting impression on your audience. That's the power of confident communication. It fosters leadership qualities, opens up new opportunities, and amplifies relationships. It can transform your personal life, making you happier and more content with who you are.

Confidence also plays an integral role in professional settings. It boosts your ability to negotiate, provide feedback, lead a team, and interact with clients. Essentially, confident communication allows you to build trust quickly, inspire others, maintain transparency, and cultivate a healthy work culture.

4.5. Disarming Fear, Embracing Confidence

Sometimes, fear holds back your power of confident self-expression. Everyone faces fear, but successful people master the art of combating it with courage and perseverance. It boils down to not letting fear dominate your mindset, to let your self-confidence shine through instead.

Start small. Maybe share an idea in a team meeting, or interact more with your colleagues. Gradually, expand your comfort zone. Answer queries in a town hall session, take up mini projects demanding interaction with various teams, or take a public speaking course.

Focus your mindset on growth rather than perfection, learning rather than avoiding mistakes. Fear is inevitable, but letting it dictate your self-expression isn't. With time, you'll learn to express yourself more freely, and as you grow, remember - your unique communication is your key to commanding confidence in the modern world.

Armed with these insights, it's clear that confident self-expression is not a gift bestowed upon a lucky few. It is, rather, a talent that can be developed with dedication and practice. Harboring it not only solidifies your personal relationships but also multiplies your possibilities of professional success.

Whichever route you take, always remember - your voice matters. It makes you who you are. Make it heard. Make it bold. Make it confident.

Chapter 5. Leveraging Empathy: Understanding Others for Better Interaction

Every successful journey of communication begins with understanding others. The role of empathy in honing our communication skills cannot be overstated. It's an inherent quality, an invisible bridge that connects us with others, which, when leveraged, can significantly improve our interpersonal interactions. This chapter emphasizes understanding and utilizing empathy for more effective communication.

5.1. The Essence of Empathy

Empathy, often mistaken for sympathy, is a feeling of understanding and sharing someone else's emotions or experiences. It is essentially 'walking a mile in somebody else's shoes' before forming judgments or taking actions. Let's separate it from sympathy; while sympathy elicits a desire to help in the face of difficulties, empathy allows us to relate to the other person's feelings on a much deeper level. Empathy implies a much higher level of emotional understanding, which in turn aids in smoother and more rewarding communication.

5.2. Cultivating Empathy: The Journey Begins Within

The first step towards cultivating empathy lies not in understanding others, but in understanding ourselves. Emotional self-awareness forms the nucleus of our empathic abilities. This ain't easy, but by analyzing our emotions, we can better empathize with similar feelings in others. Personal introspection, meditation, and journaling can all be effective tools at this stage. Once we are aware of our emotional responses, we can begin to manage them in a healthier way, which is key to developing empathy.

5.3. Empathetic Listening: A Cornerstone of Empathetic Communication

One of the most substantial steps toward communicating empathetically is empathetic listening, an approach to listen and respond to others that improves mutual understanding and trust. Empathetic listening goes beyond hearing; it absorbs the context, nonverbal cues, emotions, and points of view.

It involves not just understanding the content of what is said, but also capturing the emotions behind it. Techniques for empathetic listening can include restating and reflecting on what you have heard to show understanding, respecting the speaker's perspective even if you don't agree, and being mindful not to interrupt.

5.4. Non-Verbal Cues: Silent Empathy

Non-verbal cues constitute a significant portion of our communication. Actions, after all, speak louder than words. By being more attuned to another's body language, facial expressions, and other non-verbal cues, we can glean unspoken emotions and feelings, fostering a deeper connection.

5.5. The Benefits of Empathy

Harnessing empathy and incorporating it into the fabric of our communication has several advantages. Apart from yielding better conversations, it leads to stronger relationships and fosters an environment of respect and understanding. Not only does this humanize us, but it also makes us more approachable, affording us more influence and impact in our interactions.

5.6. Empathy: A Tool, Not a Solution

It's essential to note that while empathy is a potent tool, it doesn't guarantee resolution of conflicts or achievement of success. It's a door that lets us in, a bridge that helps us cross, but it's up to us to constructively resolve conflicts and navigate towards success.

Our capacity for empathy, the ability to understand and share the feelings of others, is inherent. However, to leverage it effectively in our communication, we need to consciously develop it. Remember, successful communication isn't about always winning; it's about understanding.

Chapter 6. The Secrets of Influential Communication

True influence comes not from forcing others to accept your viewpoint but from truly engaging them, persuading them, and smoothly navigating the landscape of their emotions and thoughts. This chapter explores the secrets of influential communication through the lens of successful individuals, aiming to arm you with the tools you need to revolutionize your interactions.

6.1. The Art and Power of Active Listening

Active listening is one of the primary pillars of influential communication. It is more than just hearing the words that are being spoken. It's about understanding the complete message, including the underlying emotions, intentions, and insights.

To engage in active listening:

1. Understand that it's not about you: Be fully present in the conversation, letting go of your self-centered mind.

2. Empathize: Empathy allows you to connect with the speaker on a profound level, enabling us to understand their feelings and perspectives.

3. Paraphrase and confirm: Bring validation to your conversations by paraphrasing the speaker's thoughts and seeking their confirmation. This not only shows respect but also clarifies any misinterpretations right there.

4. Right body language: Your non-verbal cues can demonstrate your attentiveness. Maintain eye contact, nod at appropriate times, and lean in slightly to show your engagement.

6.2. Pathways to Persuasion

Persuasion, or the art of influencing others to agree with your viewpoint, is a key facet of influential communication. Notable successful people who are excellent communicators understand and effectively employ the principles of persuasion.

1. Reciprocity: No act of kindness, however small, is ever wasted. This principle says that people are more likely to give you what you want if they receive something from you in return. In the realm of communication, this could mean offering valuable insights or information first.

2. Social Proof: People are more likely to be persuaded by things that they see others doing. An example of this in communication could be citing renowned experts or successful people who share your viewpoint.

3. Commitment and Consistency: Once people make a choice or take a stance, they will experience internal pressure to behave consistent with that commitment. You can leverage this principle by first getting small agreements from your audience prior to your main point.

4. Liking: People prefer to say yes to those they like. Building rapport and ensuring that you have a positive interpersonal connection can enhance your persuasive power.

5. Authority: People respect authority and tend to follow authoritative figures or experts. Establishing your credibility is paramount in influential communication.

6. Scarcity: Things in short supply are perceived as more valuable. Communicators can emphasize the uniqueness of their information or solution to enhance their persuasive power.

6.3. Engaging with Empathy

Empathy, or the ability to understand and share another person's experiences and emotions, is a vital tool for influential communication. Successful communicators are those who can step into another's shoes, understanding their feelings, thoughts, and experiences as though they were their own.

A few steps to enhance your empathetic communication include being fully present in conversations, prioritizing hearing over being heard, seeking to understand before seeking to be understood, and caring genuinely about the person you are communicating with.

6.4. Evoking Emotions

Emotions play a crucial role in making decisions and forming opinions. Influential communicators recognize this and are adept at engaging their audience emotionally. They use storytelling to create an emotional environment, prefer using powerful emotion-triggering words, and synchronize their own emotions with those of their audiences.

Long-lasting influence is more about emotional connection than logical argument. By tapping into the power of emotions, you create a bridge between yourself and your audience that makes it easier for your message to journey across.

Finally, never underestimate the role of perseverance. Great communicators are not individuals who got it right the first time. They stumbled, tried again, learned from their mistakes, and kept on improving. So, don't be afraid to experiment, shape, simplify, amplify and perfect your craft. In the ocean of transformation, every stroke leads you closer to the shore of success. Gradually, you will find your voice resonating, reaching further, and ringing truer.

Chapter 7. Active Listening: The Key to Meaningful Dialogues

The ability to listen, truly listen, is a skill that many lack. In a world where everyone is vying for attention, where information is overflowing, we have forgotten the art of truly listening. We listen to respond, not to understand. Active Listening is a skill that can solve this conundrum; it is the key to meaningful dialogues, significant relationships, and potent communication.

7.1. The Concept of Active Listening

Active Listening is not merely the act of hearing, it comprises the conscious absorption and decoding of spoken words, non-verbal cues, emotions, and underlying messages. It involves giving your undivided attention, clarifying the speaker's words, and offering apt replies. This process is a bridge that connects communication gaps, ensuring that information is received precisely as it is intended.

Applying Active Listening, we uphold respect for the speaker, identifying and making sense of their perspective and emotional state. It shifts the focus from simply responding and being heard to understanding and evaluating the thoughts and sentiments expressed by the speaker.

7.2. The Mechanics of Active Listening

The art of Active Listening involves a sequence of three steps: comprehend, retain, and respond.

Firstly, comprehension necessitates focusing one hundred percent on the speaker, not allowing your thoughts, judgments, or distractions to interfere. Watch their facial expressions and body language for unspoken messages. Don't interrupt or get defensive; rather, open your mind, with patience and empathy.

Next comes retention. The human mind often tends to forget what it hears, especially when communication extends over longer durations. Numerous methods, such as repeating the information mentally or jotting points down, can aid retention.

Lastly, offering thoughtful responses confirms your understanding. To form meaningful dialogues, your answer should encapsulate your comprehension and any questions or thoughts the conversation sparks.

7.3. Practical Techniques for Active Listening

Even though Active Listening takes time and practice, cultivating this habit could unveil heights of success you'd never anticipated. Here are a few techniques to enhance your Active Listening skills:

- ^Show that you're attentive:^ Regularly employing verbal indications like "aha", "ok", "uh-huh", or simply nodding your head, can reassure the speaker of your active engagement.

- ^Rephrase or summarise what you hear:^ This action assures the speaker that their words have been understood correctively. By doing so, you can create a platform for deeper discussion.

- ^Ask insightful questions:^ This gives the speaker a chance to elucidate their ideas, emotions, or viewpoints. It also gives them an understanding that you're genuinely interested in their conversation.

7.4. The Power of Silence in Active Listening

Silence, in conversation, is equally powerful as words. As an active listener, embrace pauses and don't rush to fill them. By not intervening with your reply immediately after the speaker has stopped, you're offering them a chance to gather their thoughts and delve deeper into the topic.

Furthermore, silence provides an opportunity for you to digest what's being said, consider its implications, and form thoughtful, responsive queries or comments.

7.5. The Impact of Non-Verbal Cues

Non-verbal communication encompasses facial expressions, body language, tone of voice, timing, and even silence. These can reveal feelings or thoughts that words may fail to express. Active listeners take note of these cues to catch unnoticed messages, unravel hidden emotions, and understand the speaker's viewpoint more comprehensively.

7.6. Mastering the Art of Paraphrasing

Paraphrasing involves restating what the speaker said using your own words. It serves two purposes: it assures the speaker about your understanding and it allows verification or clarification of the information delivered. Remember, when paraphrasing, it's crucial to concentrate on the essence rather than merely switching words or phrases.

7.7. Embracing Empathetic Listening

Empathy plays a pivotal role in Active Listening. Empathetic Listening is about seeing the world through the speaker's eyes. It means setting aside your viewpoint to understand their thoughts and feelings. It breeds trust, fosters a closer bond, and creates an environment where deep, meaningful conversations thrive.

7.8. The Road to Reaping Rewards

As you embark upon mastering the process of Active Listening, you will see relationships deepen, conflicts reduce, and clarity in communication improve. Active Listening is not only the key to becoming an exceptional communicator but also a meaningful contributor in every dialogue you become a part of. This skill would undoubtedly lead you onto a path filled with successes that once seemed out of your grasp.

In the words of Stephen R. Covey, "Most people do not listen with the intent to understand; they listen with the intent to reply." Revolutionize your habit and become the exception. Turn around your listening pattern, and you turn around your life. Difficult though it may seem at the beginning, the rewards at the end are worth it.

Chapter 8. Decoding the Magic of Persuasion and Charisma

A sense of charisma is somewhat elusive, often characterized as a magical or even mystical trait that sets certain individuals apart, magnetizing others towards them. Charisma and persuasion, considered invaluable assets on the road to success, employ cognitive pathways and emotional resonance to build bonds, inspire, influence, and create change. Yet, for how powerful these qualities are, they are not privy to the few. As a matter of fact, they are skills that can be honed and developed by anyone willing to learn.

8.1. The Science Behind Charisma

Charisma is not simply a product of physical attractiveness or innate charm, but rather is deeply rooted in a range of interpersonal skills that anyone can learn. Social scientists describe charismatic individuals as those who exude confidence, express themselves articulately, emotionally resonate with others, tell compelling stories, and possess a certain amount of physical grace. They have the ability to make others feel important, acknowledged, and seen.

Studies on charisma have identified the three key components as: presence, power, and warmth. Presence refers to one's ability to stay fully engrossed in the moment, emanating an authentic participation with any given interaction. Power, often judged by our subconscious, refers to the ability to influence the world around us, be it through financial means, intellect, skills, or physical strength. Lastly, warmth refers directly to the goodness perceived by others in us. It is often displayed through body language and behaviour that communicates genuine affection and concern towards others.

8.2. Developing Your Presence

Your charismatic journey starts with building presence. Make the conscious decision to remain present in each interaction. This starts by actively listening, rather than anticipating your own responses. Focus on understanding the speaker's perspective completely, absorbing their words and non-verbal cues actively. When it's your turn to speak, express genuine interest or appreciation of what was said before offering your response.

To master the art of presence, engage in mindfulness exercises daily. Learn to gather your wandering thoughts and bring the focus back to the current task or interaction. Also, reducing distractions helps. When in conversation, put away your phone, eliminate background noises, and give your complete and undivided attention.

8.3. Cultivating Power Through Communication

Your perception of power emanates from confidence in your abilities. This confidence is born when we are aware and proud of our skills, experiences, and values. To cultivate this, start by simply identifying your strengths and embracing them.

But confidence without communication is like a car without an engine. Optimizing our communication skills is crucial to projecting power effectively. This involves honing our verbal, non-verbal, and listening efficiency. Fluent, compelling speech coupled with clear and confident body language convey a strong message to the receiver. Meanwhile, active listening helps ensure our responses are constructive and relevant, thus adding to the impact of the conversation.

8.4. Embodying Warmth in Interactions

Projecting warmth is about showing sincerity and interest in others. Introduce genuine compliments into your conversations and pay attention to the person you are talking to, showing concern for their feelings and experiences.

Another significant aspect of warmth is empathy, which is the capacity to understand or feel what another person is experiencing. Utilise empathy to connect with others emotionally, showing that you comprehend their standpoint.

8.5. Mastering the Art of Persuasion

Powerful persuasion is not about manipulation or deceit. It's about presenting your thoughts or ideas in an appealing and understandable way that others find valuable and wish to align with.

To be persuasive, you must first thoroughly understand your audience. Knowing their interests, values, and language is key to forming an impactful connection. Secondly, structuring your arguments effectively is vital. Begin with a clear thesis, followed by well-researched supporting points, then sum up with a compelling conclusion.

8.6. Harnessing Storytelling for Impact

Storytelling is an integral part of charismatic speaking. It allows us to engage with the listener's emotions, making the message more memorable. Thus, the ability to weave your ideas and messages into relatable, captivating stories will significantly enhance your influence on others. To become a charismatic storyteller, embrace your unique experiences and voice. Deliver your stories with enthusiasm and varied tonality that carry the listener through the emotional arc of your narrative.

Remember, charisma and persuasion are not about selfish gain, but about forging meaningful connections and influencing positive change. As you implement these principles, anticipate progress, not perfection. Strive for growth and allow your authentic personality to shine through. Repeat these actions until they become as natural as breathing.

Only then can we truly say – you have decoded the magic of persuasion and charisma.

Chapter 9. Techniques for Difficult Conversations: Turning Tensions into Triumphs

Conflict and misunderstanding can plague any interaction, even amongst successful people. What differentiates them, however, is their ability to navigate these conversations and flip the script on discord, ensuring tensions are turned into triumphs. This chapter will cover various techniques that, when applied, can enhance your conversations, especially when they're challenging or tension-filled.

9.1. Understanding the Nature of Difficult Conversations

Before diving into the techniques involved in handling tough dialogues, it's essential to understand just what makes a conversation difficult. In essence, a demanding discussion — in personal life, professional circles, or otherwise — is any conversation that involves clashing perspectives, heightened emotions, and high stakes, often accompanied by a significant threat to self-identity.

Recognizing these elements forms the bedrock for utilizing the tactics outlined in this chapter, enabling you to navigate these choppy waters with grace and effectiveness.

9.2. Building Empathy as a Communication Bridge

One of the most potent tools you can wield in a difficult conversation is empathy. This powerful ally allows you to see the situation from the other person's perspective without necessarily agreeing with them. It establishes a sense of mutual understanding, often cooling tempers and allowing logical, reasonable discussions to prevail.

Practice active listening. This ability requires making sure the other person feels heard and genuinely trying to understand their point of view. Nodding and repetitive confirmations can affirm your engagement, while questions attempting to recast or clarify their views can demonstrate your intent to comprehend their stance fully.

9.3. Framing the Conversation

How you approach a challenging dialogue can set the tone for the entire interaction. Instead of placing blame or pointing fingers, frame the conversation around the issue instead of the person. Aim to keep your language positive, focusing on what can be done rather than what can't.

Speak from your perspective, using "I" statements like "I feel" or "I think" to convey your thoughts and feelings. Doing so can help you avoid laying blame, thus reducing the defensive attitudes that can flare up in response.

9.4. Calming the Storm: Managing Emotions

Emotions can run high during difficult conversations, and knowing how to manage them can significantly impact the outcome. Both your own emotions and those of the other party can ignite or settle the situation.

Practice emotional regulation techniques such as deep breathing exercises and taking pauses before responding to heated comments. This can maintain a balanced and calm atmosphere, allowing for a more productive dialogue.

Take your and the other party's emotional temperature regularly. Gauge feelings and adjust your approach accordingly. If you perceive that the other party is getting upset or defensive, it might be beneficial to slow the conversation down or take a break.

9.5. Assertive Capitulation

This oxymoronic technique involves maintaining assertiveness while also showing willingness to back down when required. It's all about keeping your self-respect intact while also valuing the relationship. You must remain steadfast in communicating your boundaries and expectations, yet flexible enough to negotiate and find common ground.

Remember, compromise isn't a sign of defeat, but the bedrock of functioning relationships and fruitful conversations.

9.6. Reframing the Argument

Another strategy involves reframing the argument. This act entails actively changing the conversation's context or direction by choosing an alternative perspective. It's an effective method for transforming a potential battleground into a peaceful resolution platform.

Try to identify shared goals or common values that could help shift the exchange from a win-lose scenario to a win-win situation. Plus, diverging from wanting to be "right" to prioritizing resolution can transform your conversation's trajectory.

Each of these techniques requires practice and patience. However, as you start incorporating them into your interactions, you'll notice immediate and profound benefits. Your conversations will lead towards more solutions, and the path towards your own personal reinvention will become smoother. We learn about ourselves through the reflections of others, and by expertly managing difficult conversations, you can continue shaping the successful person you're destined to be.

In the next chapter, we will explore ways to further reinforce these skills. Because the key to success doesn't just involve handling difficult conversations, it also involves defining your terms of success. We hope you will join us on this exploration of how powerful communication can shape your life.

Chapter 10. Nurturing Relationships through Constructive Feedback

Feedback is the crucible in which relationships are forged, shaped, and ultimately refined. Constructive feedback serves as the sustenance needed to nurture and grow relationships in every aspect of life. In this pursuit, truly successful people adopt an approach that is both considerate and impactful.

10.1. Identifying the Need for Constructive Feedback

Before engaging in the process of providing feedback, one must first understand its necessity. It's important to pinpoint specific areas where improvement or changes are required. These instances might involve poor performance, miscommunications, or instances where our actions, or those of our counterparts, didn't yield the desired results. In such moments, step back, analyze the situation, and identify the key areas where constructive feedback can foster growth and improvement. To execute this effectively, one should practice empathy, observational skills, and sincere understanding.

10.2. Formulating Feedback Effectively

When it comes to feedback, the presentation is as vital as the message. It would be beneficial to apply the SBI model (Situation, Behaviour, Impact), a widely used structure for providing feedback that is clear, concise, and devoid of personal biases.

1. Situation: Initiate by presenting the scenario in an objective manner. This includes where and when the incident occurred.

2. Behaviour: Specify the actions or behaviour that need attention. Be descriptive and avoid vague or generalized comments.

3. Impact: Explain the effect of the behaviour on the project, team, or individual. This cultivates an understanding of why the behaviour needs change.

The SBI model prevents the feedback from feeling like a personal attack, thus allowing the receiver to be receptive.

10.3. The Right Time and Place

Timing and setting can significantly impact the feedback process. Choosing the right time fosters receptivity while also ensuring full attention. The environment needs to be private to safeguard the confidentiality of the conversation. Successful people recognize these subtle yet crucial cues, optimizing them to bolster the efficacy of feedback.

10.4. Shielding Relationships from Harsh Criticisms

While honesty is paramount, bluntness can often bruise feelings and strain relationships. The goal is to foster progress, not inflict emotional distress. A popular method to achieve this balance is the Sandwich Feedback technique, which involves 'sandwiching' the negative feedback between two positive feedbacks. This technique helps ease the receiver into the critique while also ending the conversation on a positive note.

10.5. Receiving Feedback With Grace

Giving feedback is only half the journey–receiving feedback equally contributes to the nurturing of relationships. Ego and defensive mechanisms often act as barriers to receiving constructive feedback. Highly successful people comprehend this tendency and proactively invite feedback. Embracing vulnerability, they dismantle these barriers, fostering a culture of open communication and collective growth.

10.6. Fostering Continual Improvement

Feedback is not a one-time event, rather a process fostering continual improvement. It's about providing the right feedback at the right time and regularly, not just during formal evaluations. Keep the feedback relevant and timely, focusing on recent events rather than past actions.

10.7. Concluding Thoughts

The process of feedback, both giving and receiving, is a delicate dance that requires emotional intelligence, tact, and patience. Wielding this tool effectively can nurture relationships, fostering a culture of growth and continuous improvement. Remember, feedback is a gift, and imparting it constructively can contribute positively to the personal and professional growth of your peers. Similarly, receiving it with grace, a learning mindset, and an openness to adapt can be your pathway to self-improvement and success.

With practice, patience, and sincere commitment, this dance of giving and receiving feedback can become your secret weapon in nurturing relationships that not only survive but thrive in professionalism, mutual respect, and unwavering support. Relationships that are rooted in honesty, nurtured by feedback, and cultivated with mutual respect can withstand the tests of time, tread the waters of change, and ultimately, redefine the paradigms of success.

Chapter 11. Final Thoughts: Integrating Communication Skills into Your Daily Life

Upon reflecting upon the key communication skills of highly successful people, the importance of assimilating these skills into one's daily life cannot be overstated. It is not enough to know about them; it is crucial to live them. Thus, this chapter aims to guide you on how to incorporate these transformative communication concepts into your everyday existence.

11.1. The Art of Active Listening

Listening is an essential skill in communication, but we often overlook its importance. Active listening involves more than just hearing what someone is saying, but engaging with them at a deep level with minimal judgement.

To integrate active listening into your life, start by practicing focused attention. This could be by minimizing distractions when having a conversation. Also, keep in mind that it's not just the words that matter but the non-verbal cues as well. Are their arms folded over their chest signifying they might be defensive? Or are their eyes animated, indicating excitement? These small details are just as important in understanding the message someone is trying to convey.

Remember, active listening demands giving feedback. Show that you understand what's being said by asking insightful questions, summarizing their points, and not interrupting.

11.2. Persuasion: A Tool for Influence

Persuasion, another significant communication skill, allows us to influence others. This isn't about manipulation, rather it's about aligning our goals with those of others. You can start using persuasion in your life in small ways. Next time you're discussing where to have lunch with friends, use the persuasion skills you've learned to align your choice with theirs.

Remember, when persuading, it's always crucial to be respectful of the values, beliefs, and perspectives of others. Understand and appreciate where they're coming from, and that will make your persuasion more productive and less confrontational.

11.3. Ability of Concise Communication

Conciseness is not about simply being brief, but about including all necessary points in the most efficient manner possible. To incorporate this into your daily life, practice summarizing complex ideas into simple and crisp sentences.

For example, if you find an interesting article online, try to summarize it in a tweet or a written paragraph. Keep doing this regularly until it becomes second nature. The key here is to express maximum meaning with minimum words without losing essential information.

11.4. Empathy: The Power to Connect

Empathy is the ability to understand others' feelings from their perspectives. It involves being sensitive to their emotions, and acting in ways that showcase this understanding and concern.

To practice empathy daily, try putting yourself in other people's shoes before responding in any situation. For instance, if a friend shares a problem with you, try to imagine how you would feel if it were happening to you. This helps champion empathetic communication.

11.5. Assertiveness: Advocating for Your Views

Assertiveness refers to the ability to stand up for one's views in a respectful and confident manner. Balancing assertiveness is tricky; too little and you might be overlooked, too much and you could come off as aggressive.

As a daily exercise, practice stating your opinions and needs clearly and respectfully. It could be as simple as expressing your food preferences at a restaurant or more complex like stating your viewpoint in a heated discussion.

Integrating communication skills into your daily life is not a one-and-done task, it's a journey. You might stumble along the way, but it's important to remember the end goal. Success rarely comes in leaps and bounds; it's a series of small steps that eventually compound into noticeable and remarkable transformation.